BIRDS of PREY

BIRDS of PREY

GLENDA POWELL OLSEN

THE CHILD'S WORLD

Eagles 8

Hawks 10

Harriers 12

Ospreys 14

Kites 16

Falcons 18

Caracaras 20

Condors 22

Vultures 24

Buzzards 26

Secretary Birds 28

Owls 30

Imagine a quiet, sunny day on a large lake. Suddenly, a shadow appears. In a heartbeat, a bald eagle dives toward the water's surface. Barely slowing down, the powerful bird reaches underwater, snatches a large fish, and flies off to enjoy its feast from a favorite perch.

Eagles belong to a group of large birds called birds of prey, or *raptors*. About 400 species of raptors exist, all highly skilled hunters. They prey on many animals, including insects, fish, mammals, reptiles, and even other birds. All raptors are armed with excellent eyesight, hooked beaks, strong legs, and very sharp claws, or *talons*.

Many birds of prey are abundant, but others are threatened with extinction. Unfortunately, humans are these birds' greatest enemies. Pollution, population growth, and illegal hunting are the primary threats to their survival. Let's visit some of these fascinating birds in the forests, mountains, shorelines, and deserts where they soar.

EAGLES

Eagles live in forests and open plains, often nesting on rocky cliffs. They have broad wings that are excellent for soaring. The emblem of the United States, the bald eagle, is not actually bald—it has stark-white feathers covering its head. The bird's talons are very strong and sharp, perfect for plucking fish out of the water. Eagles have corrective vision, so reflections on the water do not interfere with their aim. Bald eagles mate for life and use the same nest year after year to raise their young. The largest nests are the size of a small car!

HAWKS

Although they are often mistaken for eagles, hawks are generally smaller. They are also more talented flyers. Known for their speed and agility, these raptors are sometimes trained as hunting birds. Most hawks live in wooded areas, often near water. Some species have knees that bend both ways! This comes in handy when the birds want to reach their young, which live in hollow trees. It's pretty useful for nabbing afternoon snacks, too! Some female hawks choose more than one male to complete their families.

HARRIERS

Harriers are close relatives of hawks, but they look more like owls. These birds hover over the ground, searching for food, then drop quickly to make the kill. Harriers like to snack on small mammals, birds, insects, and reptiles. Their acute hearing helps them detect prey. Harriers really put on a show at mealtime! The male doesn't return to the nest with the food he's caught. Instead, the female flies up to him, turns upside down, then catches the food as the male drops it! Unlike most other raptors, harriers often nest close to the ground.

OSPREYS

Ospreys live near rivers, swamps, or other bodies of water. They often spend the winters in warm, tropical regions but breed in cooler climates. The osprey's camouflaged coloring—dark on top and white underneath—is imitated on many warplanes. Also known as fishing hawks, ospreys snatch fish by plunging feet-first into the water. The bird's long, sharp talons ensure a good grip on even the most slippery fish. An osprey's grip is so good, in fact, that large fish sometimes pull the birds underwater and take them for a swim!

KITES

Compared to other birds of prey, kites are relatively small. Of the thirty-one species of kites, the smallest is only twelve inches long. Kites live in marshy habitats on every continent except Antarctica. These raptors live in large colonies but prefer to hunt alone. One of the rarest raptors is the Everglades kite. Talk about fussy eaters! Only one kind of snail appeals to these finicky critters. So much for a balanced diet! Other, more common kites are red, black, and letter-winged kites—all of which are much easier to please at mealtime.

FALCONS

Falcons live in open, grassy regions of every continent except Antarctica. Unlike other birds of prey, falcons do not build their own nests. Instead, they use hollow trees or nests abandoned by other birds. Exceptional fliers, falcons often snatch small birds—their favorite meal—right out of the air! In the Middle Ages, nobles trained peregrine falcons to hunt other birds. This sport, called *falconry*, is still popular in some parts of the world. When diving for a kill, peregrine falcons can reach speeds of over 200 miles per hour!

CARACARAS

Though related to falcons, caracaras are the rude relatives that no one wants to claim. These long-legged birds make their homes in Central and South America. A variety of foods, including decaying animals, or *carrion*, satisfy their taste buds. Rather lazy, these birds spend most of their time perched. Occasionally they go for walks. Completely lacking manners, caracaras often intrude on carrion discovered by other birds. Not only do they take over the carcass, they even force the earlier diners to disgorge their food!

CONDORS

With its seventeen-foot wingspan, the Andean condor of South America is the largest flying bird in the world. Its close relative, the California condor, is one of the most endangered of all birds. In fact, there are only about thirty California condors left alive. The birds' decline has resulted partly from their diet. Condors eat carrion, which often contains poison. The poison accumulates in a condor's body, eventually killing the bird. To make matters worse, condors feed their young by regurgitation, so the chicks absorb the poison, too.

VULTURES

Unlike most raptors, vultures do not have strong claws or sharp talons, so they cannot kill their own prey. Instead, they search for dead or dying animals. They float on rising air currents, conserving energy by flapping their large wings only when necessary. The birds sometimes travel ninety miles or more to track a meal. Imagine driving that far to find a McDonald's! Once a vulture spots a carcass, other vultures in the area soon notice. The resulting flocks can completely devour an adult zebra in a matter of minutes!

BUZZARDS

There are more than fifty species of buzzard living in Europe, Asia, and Africa. These versatile birds thrive in many different habitats—from tropical forests to frozen tundra. Buzzards feed primarily on small mammals and other birds. Buzzards' flying skills rival those of nearly any bird. They often soar without flapping their large, outstretched wings. Many species put on elaborate dances in the sky, performing loops, figure-eights, and cartwheels. The birds put on these displays to attract mates, show off, or just plain have fun!

SECRETARY BIRDS

Standing over three feet tall, the long-legged secretary bird lives only in Africa. These birds are named for the long feathers on the back of their necks that resemble quill pens. Oddly enough, the birds also have two tail feathers with black "ink spots." Unlike other raptors, secretary birds have short, stubby toes that are designed for walking, not grasping prey. It's not surprising that this bird doesn't find its food in the water or in the air. Instead, it walks along the ground, hunting insects, small rodents, and sometimes snakes.

OWLS

Owls differ from all other raptors because they are active at night, or *nocturnal*. Of the 133 species of owls, the largest is 100 times bigger than the smallest. Even so, all owls have the same distinct facial disks and large heads. Owls are known for their keen eyesight, but they rely mainly on their acute hearing when hunting. As with the rest of the raptor family, the female is larger than the male. Barn owls, which hunt mice, might be the farmer's best friend! Some farmers cut small openings in their barns so the birds can get in and out.

PHOTO RESEARCH

Charles Rotter/Archipelago Productions

PHOTO CREDITS

COMSTOCK/Phyllis Greenberg: 27

COMSTOCK/Russ Kinne: 19

Joe McDonald: 4, 15, 17, 21, 25, 29, 31

Thomas Mangelsen: 11

Tom and Pat Leeson: front cover, 7, 9

VIREO/B.K. Wheeler: 13

Westlight/Charles Philip: 2, 23

Library of Congress Cataloging-in-Publication Data
Olsen, Glenda Powell.
Birds of prey / by Glenda Powell Olsen.
p. cm.
Summary: Describes the physical characteristics and habits
of such birds of prey as ospreys, falcons, vultures, and eagles.
ISBN 1-56766-059-2
1. Birds of prey--Juvenile literature.   [1. Birds of prey.]
I. Title.

QL696.F30385   1993   93-2670
598.9'1--dc20

Distributed to schools and libraries in the United States by:
ENCYCLOPAEDIA BRITANNICA EDUCATIONAL CORP.
310 South Michigan Avenue
Chicago, Illinois 60604